Daily Yoga

For a Happy and Healthy Cat

By Shri Swami Sattvapurrrrrananda

Photography by Julianne Victoria

Daily Yoga for a Happy and Healthy Cat

Copyright 2013 by Julianne Victoria and Through the Peacock's Eyes Press

All rights reserved. This book may not be reproduced in whole or part, stored in retrieval system or transmitted in any form or by any means – electronic, mechanical, or other – without written permission from the publisher, except by a reviewer, who may quote brief passages in a review.

www.peacockseyes.com

Introduction

To all my fellow felines:

As you all well know, cats, being one of the highest life forms and possessing great insight and wisdom, are natural yogis. However, many of us are all too often caught up in the fast pace and stress of the modern world, so I felt that it was my dharma to take upon this selfless karmic act and put together a simple, yet thorough guide for a daily yoga practice. I have chosen for this book the most vital and harmonizing Asana and Pranayama that will lead to a long, healthy, and joyful life for all.

May you all find bliss and peace within!

"If one stretches completely, one relaxes completely. Look at a cat, a master of stretching and a master of relaxation."

                                                                    -B.K.S. Iyengar, <u>Light on Life</u>

Preparation

There are just a few things a yogicat needs to begin a yoga practice: a suitable location and a few props. A soft, comfortable blanket, towel, or any pleasing surface will do. Although a quiet environment is ideally desired, a yogicat living in a meditative state of awareness and calm will discover that they are quite easily able to practice in almost any environment. Props, such as stuffed mice, can be useful for getting into and staying in some of the more challenging positions, but are not required.

Keeping the body clean inside and outside is an important part of living a yogic lifestyle. Regular bathing and adequate hydration and nutrition are necessary to cleanse and nourish our perfectly beautiful feline temples!

My most common yoga practice location: my yoga blanket with some of my props. I usually lay my blanket across the couch to protect the joints.

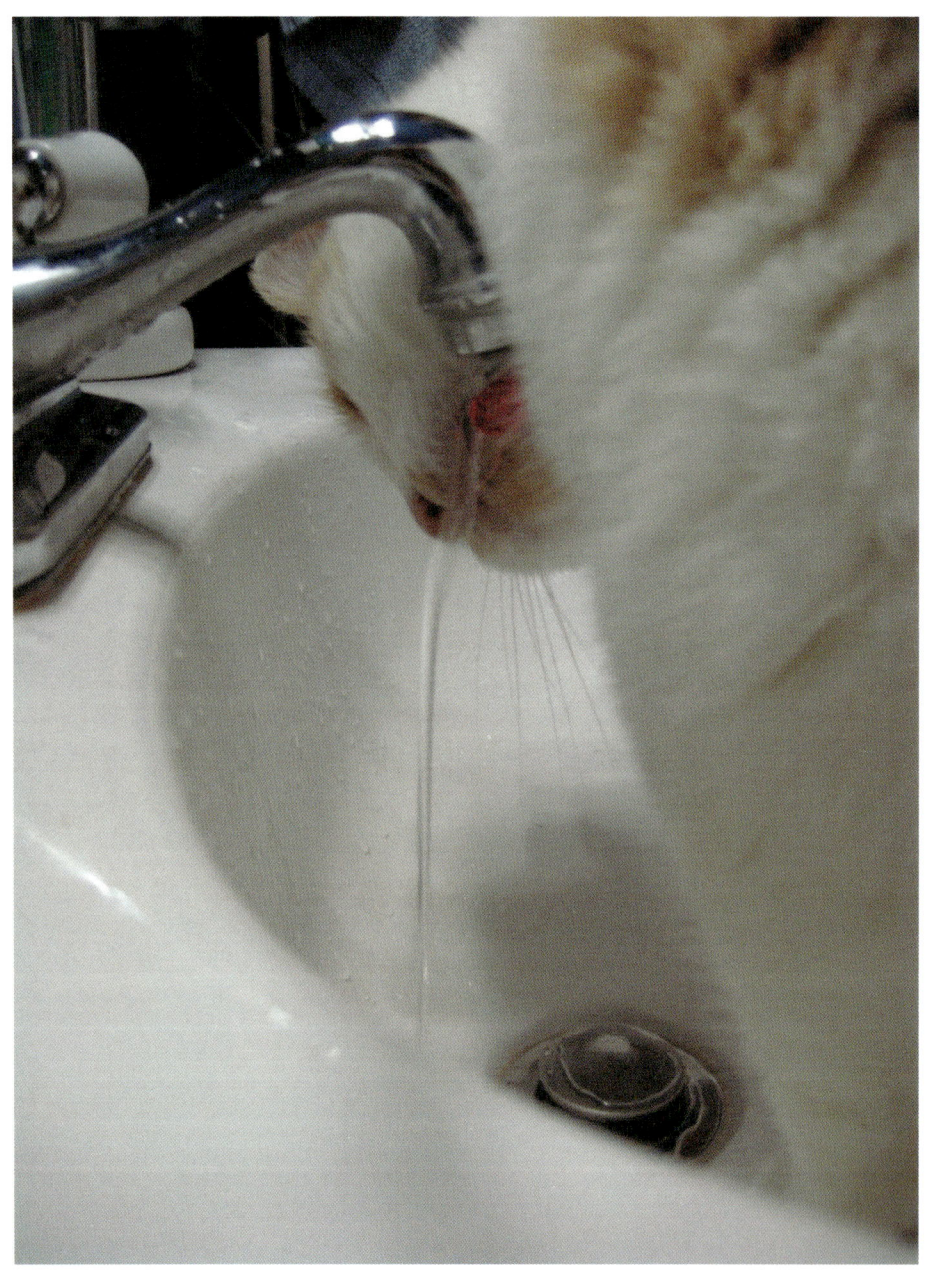

Running water is especially refreshing and invigorating! I try to drink fresh running water as often as possible.

Asana

Balasana (kitten pose):

In Balasana, hind legs are tucked under and front legs are at one's side. Head is in a rested position, with either the forehead up or down. Here, as in any pose, you may wrap yourself in a blanket if you feel a chill. This is an excellent Asana when doing an hours-long meditation!

Sphinx Asana (Sphinx pose):

With abdomen and hind legs grounded, and front legs extended comfortably, lift head and heart. Here I have used one of my props to keep my tail in a properly curved position. Sphinx pose brings confidence and poise.

Parivritta Sphinx Asana (revolved Sphinx pose):

Revolved Sphinx pose is a wonderful way to open the upper Chakras after a good night's sleep. To get into revolved Sphinx pose, begin in Parsvashavasana (see page 17), which you may already be in if you have just woken up. Rotate your upper body into an upright position. Front legs are extended, and head and heart lifted.

Supta Vyaghrasana (reclining tiger pose):

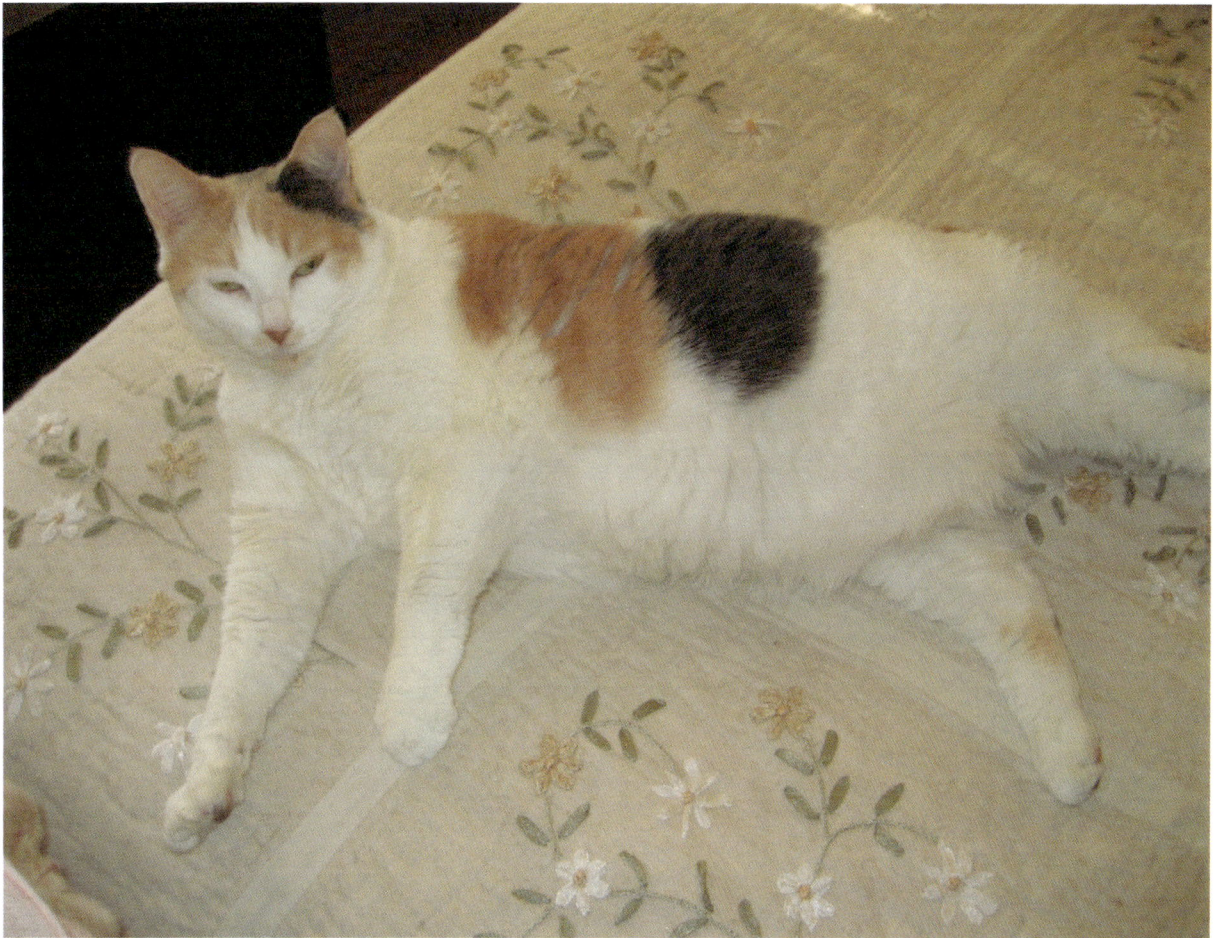

This pose brings me back to my days as a Bengal tiger! Begin in the side reclining position. Then extend one hind leg back behind you. Remember to do both legs on both sides. This is a very nice pose to do before getting up to go outside for some quiet walking meditation!

Simhasana & Simhagarjanasana (lion & roaring lion poses):

Simhasana is a lovely pose for lengthening and bringing stability to our most agile spines. It's a great way to start the day or open up to the sun after a long nap!

Simhagarjanasana is done in the same position. Just let out a few stress-relieving roars. This will open up the jaw, throat, and lungs, which is very beneficial if you chose to add some chanting to your practice. Me-Om is my favorite mantra.

Anandamarjari Asana (happy cat pose):

This is an excellent pose for resting the spine and opening up the abdomen. Just lie on your back with legs up. The state of bliss this pose brings can be accentuated by gently rocking from side to side.

Supta Marjari Asana (reclining cat pose):

I believe cat pose is self-explanatory. Here I have shown it in the preferred reclining position. Reclining cat pose can be held for several hours!

Supta Padahastasana (reclining paw-paw pose):

This is a pleasing pose that strengthens the abdominal muscles and opens up the space between the shoulder blades. As you reach your front paws towards your back paws, contract your core. Supta Padahastasana is nice to do before resting in one of the variations of Shavasana.

Shavasana (corpse pose):

With hind legs stretched out and front legs in a relaxed position, let your body rest.

Shavasana is another great pose for practicing very deep meditation.

Parsvashavasana (side corpse pose):

A great pose for opening up the sides. Here I have performed Parsvashavasana on the firmer surface of the coffee table to accentuate the opening of the ribcage.

Advasana (reverse corpse pose):

Advasana is a wonderful pose for opening up the back of the neck. I often do this pose after spending many contemplative hours looking up and connecting with the divine energy of the sun. Lie down with legs resting at your sides with chin tucked in and face down.

Pranayama

Purrra Pranayama (purr breathing):

This is such a beautifully divine and natural breathing practice for cats that there are no words to describe this pleasant hum that is representative of the hum of the Universe. Purrra Pranayama always lifts the corners of one's mouth towards the sky!

Seektari Pranayama (hissing breathing):

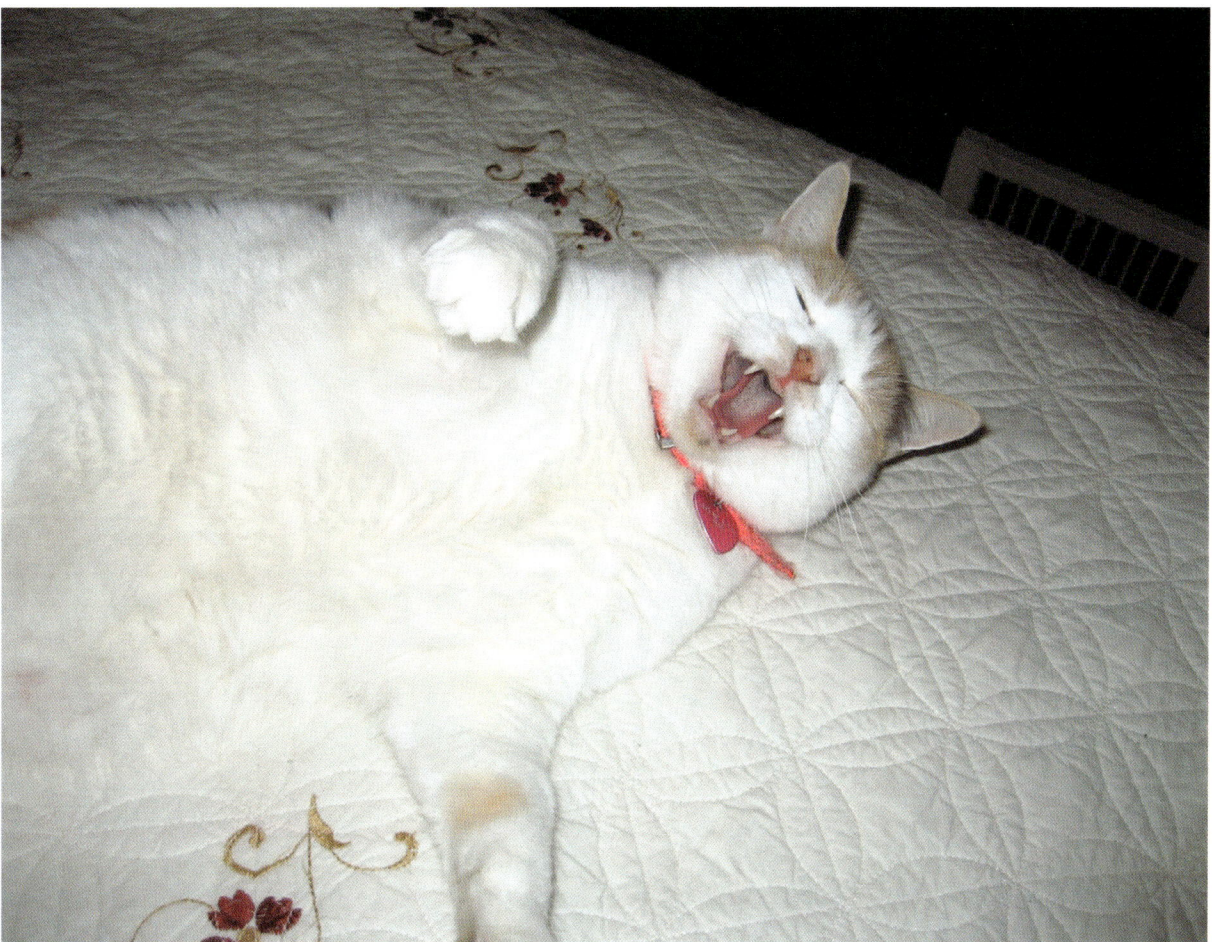

Seektari Pranayama is well known for cooling the body and the mind. Most felines practice hissing breathing when mentally heated, but its physical benefits should not be ignored. With tongue curled and lips pulled back, let out a strong force of hot air. Ahhh...makes one instantly feel calmer and cooler!

Conclusion

It has been a great joy and selfless effort to provide my fellow felines with an essential guide to yoga. The Asana and Pranayama addressed in this book may be practiced in any sequence and combination, and for any duration. Though some of these poses may seem daunting at first, I am confident that in no time at all, you will be able to perform all of them with great ease.

With Love,

Shri Swami Sattvapurrrrrananda

About the Author

For thousands of lifetimes (yes, there are more than nine lives!), Shri Swami Sattvapurrrrrananda has had the blessing of being reincarnated as a cat. She thanks Brahma, Vishnu, and Shiva for guiding her through the cycles of life, and for giving her this extraordinary opportunity to be of service to all felines, big and small.

In her current incarnation, Swami resides in San Francisco, California where she has made yoga her constant practice. She thanks her family for their support of her tireless efforts to perfect her yoga practice.

"Practice becomes firmly grounded when well attended to for a long time, without break and in all earnestness."

The Yoga Sutra's of Patanjali I:14

Sri Swami Satchidananda

Made in the USA
San Bernardino, CA
30 May 2013